WHAT

WE

DID

TO

HER

MADE

THE

WATER

RISE

What We Did To Her Made The Water Rise

Meghann Plunkett

BLACK LAWRENCE PRESS

Black Lawrence Press

Executive Editor: Diane Goettel
Chapbook Editor: Lisa Fay Coutley
Book Cover and Interior Design: Zoe Norvell
Cover Artwork: *Liminal XIII* by Yang Cao

ISBN: 978-1-62557-164-9

Published 2024 by Black Lawrence Press.
Printed in the United States.

Table of Contents

Gaslight

We lived above a butcher shop and each morning men with blood
      on their aprons would unload inventory
from a dented truck. They were doing this just for me. No, they were
      not. That year, I wilted in the smell of raw things
and a thickness twisted in from our only window that tunneled the day

onto our damp, hungover noon. And the pounding of the chopping block
      in brutal intervals rattled up through the pipes
of our apartment, telling us how much time had passed in the act of piecing
      apart. I know, because there was love in the hold-down. Right? Yes.
Counting ninety bangs of the cleaver before he'd peel himself off of me.

I was all the things left over. Sometimes a bucket of snouts like rotten peaches
      thrown out in the alley and then cats, cats—worming out from under
a chain-link fence. I loved the sound of their discomfort rapturing through
      the brick-wall heat, how it was larger than my own. I don't know. Maybe
I didn't. But the room was always stinking of August. My books kept in boxes

under the bed, there was no art to the refusal of unpacking—only a way to shake
      the song from a body. A clucking of chickens until one by one:
silence. I think, anyway. All the locks in the apartment were broken that year
      and the landlord insisted the pipes were not leaking. I set coffee cups catching
a liquid the color of bone marrow. No. That year, the mail would arrive as white

as warning, as flashing teeth—each letter yellowing, unopened. And the rats alive
      in the walls had babies, moving like maggots inside the building's flesh.
Yes, that's true. The door wouldn't fix and he hit it. The hinges creaking out
      the same sound he would growl in my ear each night. And the nickel-
size bruises ripening on my thighs were not there. His name welting cursive

up my back and I liked it. I wouldn't fix. How could I
      explain my jealousy of other things he touched with his fists? How I tried
      each night to be as quiet as a bottle of whiskey—easier

to take between the lips.
     Didn't I? Each day believe
         the ending of his story
            that there wasn't anything
               other than the butcher,
                  his hands,
                     a blade—

"Waves crashing against the coastline erode until a notch is formed. The erosion of this notch undercuts the ground above it until it becomes unstable and collapses."

–Geological Survey
Department of the Environment
Climate and Communications, 2023

My mother tells me about her assault

and another storm moves up the cold side
     of our home. The wind wails like a newborn
but she sleeps through the night.
     I cradle each bag of sand into the burlap

darkness, stack them over the cellar door.
     The dishes are lifted down to the kitchen floor—
everything breakable must be taken
     out into the open. The water

rising over the seawall like a hand over a mouth.
     What barrels down our coastline wants us
dead. I hammer the windows closed and wait for it
       to surge under the front door.

The dog bowl floats toward my mother's
     bed. My ankles drown in what can't be
       kept out.

Researchers Find that Trauma is Inherited Through DNA

In a pregnant mother, three generations are directly exposed
to the same environmental conditions at the same time.
*   - Epigenetics & Inheritance Research, University of Utah*

Something about the smell of bleach. Church bells. My name
spoken too loudly. Something inside me tearing like a cheap stocking.
I was an egg inside my mother when she was still an egg inside

her mother. An angled bathroom mirror stretching into an infinity
of women. All of us learning how
to be left. My mouth stitched with all the ways we learned to be

quiet. What don't I know about the way birds fly
when startled? What don't I know about the ground
becoming an open maw? A hand up my skirt

and my hunger for what might be taken away. A spoiled
sack of organ meat echoes through the decades and becomes
a stash of cereal in my nightstand drawer. Who locked the door?

My grandmother clears her throat and I drink glass
after glass after glass. Who was it? Walking
the long way home? Shouldering away

from a car full of men? What is it about a broken radio
that pocks me into hives? Someone's fingers
bleeding the needle and thread. My hand

flies up to protect my face when the door creaks
open. Whose reflexes are these? Unable
to sleep. Listening and listening for the sound of keys.

Beyond Nature

September and everything was heavy
          with lack. The bay flooded, stinking
of sulfur. Summer crowds
          disappeared. Suddenly. A splintering
umbrella. An empty bag of chips tumbling
          into the waves. Blue crabs scuttling
with bits of plastic grown
          into their shells. The empty yawn of a gutted marsh
rippled with oil-thin rainbows.
          It was beyond nature. Surrounded by
gone. There was no one
          to guide boats into harbor from a fog-choked
cove. No one in the bait shop, closed
          after Labor Day. No fading smell of fish and rot.
No thick slabs of tuna on a bed of sharp ice. Nothing
          squirming against a glass tank. Only the empty
shack whose windows I'd hold my face to each day
          on my way to school. I'd look through to the back office
to see the women torn from magazines
          pinned up above a tide chart. One so faded she barely had a face,
her legs spread in leather chaps. Another tacked
          to the wall with a rusted nail, desperate, tied up
with rope. Her breasts popping like peeled grapes,
          a cherry gag in her mouth slick with spit. I couldn't stop. Wanting
her. No, wanting to be her. No— And it was always
          this way. It snowed too early. The corners of the photographs
curled inward. The cold came so suddenly
          it made the electricity go out. It was how we lived.
I stopped noticing at all.

Portrait of Mother as Gone

Will her ghost crave what she craves? My liquor bottles   rattling
like wind chimes. The medicine cabinet   unlatching
all by itself. My hauntings are manageable   shapes
in the form of small, white pills. Each one   placed on the tongue
is a communion and she is still here. Eyes   thrown to the back of
the head like dice into an alley.   Her name
fingered in cursive on the bathroom mirror.   I am
taking bets, confessing her memory into   the hum of a dial tone,
collecting dues paid with grief.   I am
lost without the lullaby of her constant want: an addict
to point me north. This is a part of it   too. I understand
the process of coaxing a life away from itself.   The careful surgery
of removing a sallow mind. What does the stinging   of
morning feel like without the slow tragedy of   looking
to bring the night back? What now? Give me days,   just
days and days of nothing but static. Give me empty promises   like
flowers rotting in a vase on my vanity until they smell like   her—
a body that's given up on being a body. Give me something I know.

Minnows

Once they get in, they can't figure out how to escape.
A trap meshed into a cone-shape. My father showed me

how to cast it far from the dock,
looping the twine twice around his fist.

We waited for the morning fog to lift, the sun
freckled my shoulders as I scraped my legs along

the barnacle buildup. When it was time to pull
it in, hand over hand—the trap came up, slick

with squirming. Twisting, he taught me to release
them into a bucket. A dozen bodies glinting

and flickering against the plastic pail. At the bait shop,
we lifted them onto the counter. Ten cents

for the silver-sides, fifteen for the fat-nosed.
The door to the back office swung closed as I counted

the coins. A fishermen threading a hook
through their small, saucer eyes. The next day,

I went alone. The same muddy cove. The same
casting and pulling—but this time

I took the bucket home. Wedged into the back
of my closet, the sharp cedar stung against

their metallic stink. I fed them Ritz crackers
and Cheerios. The closet door closing like

an accordion—their world dark
with my saving. And which was it? My love

for them, or my love for their rescue that kept me
peering in—reaching to feel one swim through my grasp.

The heat of the home. The dark water gone
stale. My own two hands. Them dead by morning.

When Princess Diana Died

My mother held vigil by the blue light of her television for weeks.
    Each station, on a 24 hour loop–– the princess
with her head tilted down under a crown of diamonds. Over
    and over, they panned along the masses of flowers
left to wilt along the Pont de l'Alma. It was too hot,
    even for August, and the pond outside our home
sat so still algae grew thick enough to tint the water green. No one
    could fish. The Paris police retrieved her car with the claws
of a large crane. The lights of the paparazzi glittered through our home
    as my mother blinked in disbelief. Upside down, the hood sparked
along the asphalt as it was yanked from the mouth of the tunnel. The airbags
    dragging like aging breasts and she wept—refused to eat.
Years before, my mother clipped her hair like hers. The princess
    wore a red skirt with a slit. My mother showed off her long legs
the next day. She flipped through magazines to find her, to learn
    what was allowed. *I don't understand, I don't understand,*
she opened and closed her mouth like a gutted trout, huddled by the fan,
    chewing ice cubes from a chipped glass. The royal family refused
to lower the flags. She left her husband—couldn't be honored. The palace gate
    closed with no response. *See what happens when you try*
to have your own life?

Field Trip

It was a nickel to view and our school group let us
climb on the silver viewfinders lining the river, using

the last of our lunch money to flip the binocular-eye
open to the other side of the city. Amy saw it first,

grabbing my shoulder and pulling me over, the metal
sight revealing the mouth of an alley where a woman

was bent over the hood of a car and a man behind her—
driving himself over and over.

The boy beside me pretended his viewfinder was
a machine gun, making the plosives of war—wet, loud—

his spit flying as I looked at their mouths moving
in a silent, far-off heaving. Other girls gathered behind

me, taking turns tugging at each other's plaid skirts. We
cowered together so tightly we looked like one animal—

our uniforms blending into a twelve ankled beast, hungry
to see. Amy's slack gasp exposed the gap where her new

teeth were coming in—*more* she said, her hand out flat
as I dug into my pockets for my last coin to thumb

into the machine. And the boys continued to pretend to die
or kill each other in a swarm of swinging backpacks until

a whistle blew—calling the mass of us back to the bus.
I was the last one to see the man leave, fixing the collar

of his shirt, returning to the street, leaving the woman there
to count a handful of bills.

On Keeping a Pet

& also how a box of porcelain dolls looks
        almost like one body.   Nine dresses
           flowering into one another, eighteen
arms stretched up & each claret-red mouth

        painted perfectly shut. My mother sells them
to the consignment shop for ten cents
        & a tiny dusk darkens in her girlhood. Not weeks before,
           for the first time, she woke to a startling of blood

between her legs—*I'm dying, I'm dying*—
        & her ditch-silent mother filling the bathtub
with bleach. Even the street cats in heat were bleating too
        I'm dying, I'm dying. She learned a lot

        that summer: which ways not to walk
alone at night, how to hush-up & shut
        her goddamn knees. A catholic school uniform
yanked a little lower. She started to watch
        how her own mother drew two

perfect lines up the back of her legs.
        Eyeliner disappearing up her thigh like a dirt
           road curving behind a hill. When they took her

to the barber shop, they held her shoulders & her ponytail—
        orange as a gourde—was severed at the root. She watched
           it fall from her like a rag-doll, pillowing
onto the floor. At home, she tucked the soft thing
        into her nightstand drawer—*we are all cursed*

    with something to care for—she thought
        of the tailor measuring the length
of her thigh, his hot hand reaching up into her

skirt. How she told no one
                of those nights she'd sneak outside
with a saucer of milk, stand at the mouth
        of the lightless alley—call & call & call

South County, Matunuck, RI

Each winter a new storm bent on our shoreline and damage
bloomed wild. When the neighbors left, we stayed

watching the seawall recede stone by stone. The windows
of other houses grew closed as ours glowed

through each night. Begging for it. A line corseting
our walls thinner from where the water rose and entered

through the windows. Our small peninsula of land caught
between the bay and the gray Atlantic—

there was no hope. Gulls nested on the barren island
of our roof, cracking blue crabs on battered shingles.

waves gnashed up our welcome mat. Half-crushed
minnows gasped on our doorstep. My father grinned

like a mad man when he'd wade out to get the mail.
The floating garbage barrels spinning over

and over like pigs on a spit. And then everything
grew larger around us. The school lifted

by two cranes, the church tilting on seventeen stilts,
one barn moved half an acre back. The fog horn giving up mid-

January, the lighthouse rolling its neck like a drunk. We lived
with the smell of the tide thick in our sweaters.

A pair of swans floating underneath a barnacled
swing set watching our home inch closer and closer

to the breaking of waves—chewed by salt, slowly

disappearing—my mother with her two palms pressed
to the window, fogging the glass with the small

weather of her breath.

Portrait of my Mother at Sixteen Taken for The Providence Journal

Her hair is ironed flat and oil-black against
hollowed cheekbones. She is leaning against a brick
wall, her back arching to make her breasts look

impossible. Doe-fair, eye-wide and wearing false
eyelashes—her lips open in an awe-struck *oh*.

This was the prize for being runner up
at the Miss Rhode Island beauty pageant.
A photoshoot, three outfits to take home
        and a consultation
                with a professional agent. I know the story.

The photographer asks her to undo one more button.
        The beauty consultant handles her
                jaw, profiles her face from left to right
        commenting on the scar on her nose,
using his two fingers to spread her lips
        away from her crooked teeth.

And it ends here. The photo in my hands
        as I sift through the back of her closet looking
to empty out the last of her alcohol. I find the photograph
        in a faded shoebox. I find the vodka. I drink it
myself.

Infestation

Stainless steel and strapped back, the year we were infested
and our house was riddled with traps—the bedrooms, beneath
the good couch, on the kitchen counter—creamy dollops
of peanut butter set just below the landing. It was thought best
to bring them out into the open. We saw them in pieces, their tails
disappearing behind a corner like something you could almost prove.
This must have been why the porch light was left on like we were waiting
for someone to come home, and the telephone rang once a day
with a woman's quiet breathing on the other end. My mother rushing
to the receiver asking, asking. And my father's silence grew so large
it became another child; walloping on all fours, learning the world
through its mouth. I wanted it to stop and took to setting off the traps
myself. The thick bar welting a line across my finger in the shape of a ring.
Or I'd caulk the openings in the cedar with chewing gum until a soft
scratching became the smell of sour milk—I didn't know
what I wanted. I told no one of the nest I found in the attic. Round,
damp and made from swatches of my mother's robes. Or about
the one clattering with a trap still attached to its tail like something
that thinks it's free. But it wasn't the mice that kept me coming back, it was
the photograph stuffed deep into a box grown paisley with mold. Over
and over I'd visit to see my mother, 20 years old, nude and posing in a frame
whose glass had been cracked on purpose. Her hips narrower than I
have known, her hair Farrah Fawcett big, mimicked in winged
swoops. Her two eyes dead into the camera, covering with her hands
the small V between her legs. And her breasts. I can't
say anything about them. It wasn't the shock
of her naked body. It was the smooth of her belly, the lack of stretch—no
mark left from the sectioning it took to pull me out of her. No raised
water line in the shape of a smile below her waist, nothing for her to point to
when she'd lift her shirt and say: *look, look at what you did to me.*

Columbarium

When Amy held my head underwater
              I thought of the ashes.
        For generations our family urns turned
over into the pond. The dust of us
              floating and dissolving
        into brackish water making the sandpipers
sick. It was a game—I pulled Amy's hair,
              our legs scrambling
        in a frantic treading of water. Small yelps
bloated with laughter and fear. Our new breasts hard
              against the other's back
        as we tried to sink like stones—afraid
and alive and in love with the idea
              of going too far. Thrashing
        until we couldn't breathe. It was boredom
or something more. Our small lives blimped
              with restlessness. Waves
        of foam gathering at our waistline.
And the church down the road trotted their congregation
              to the water's edge—one by one
        heads tilted backward. What more can I say
about the doom of a body?
              A lineage of women pruned into my skin.
        Pieces of them grown into the reeds.
Stuck to a heron's foot.
              A school of minnows twists
        around our struggle
as she holds me under water again—
              this time for too long.
        The muffle of my own
        voice. My world muted. My lungs,
              open and filling.

Wild and Dangerous

It was the year JonBenét was everywhere and I grew two small breasts.
    In the grocery line, her face on every magazine
        cover—a pageant gown and a crown of baby's
breath on her head—as I bought bubblegum and learned
    to pop it loud. She was on our tongues
        the way all girls' deaths seem to be. My mother shaking
her head *what a shame,* tsking at the scars
    on my legs, rubbing them with her thumb
        like a dent on an expensive car. Whenever
the neighborhood boys chased Amy and I,
    we'd slip through a hole in the boatyard
        fence to avoid them. The smell of rotting
wood damp in our hair. We practiced kissing under broken rowboats.
    We sang Mariah Carey's *Fantasy* in a weak falsetto.
        Amy showed me the pad between her legs
and the creased line of blood and I lied about mine
    that had never come. The photos of girls
        who went missing hung in the community
center, all in a line, listing the ages they'd be now: 9, 12, 18, 34.
    Braces. Smiling. Gone. My mother, dressing
        to go out on the town, wiggled into a girdle. Winking
at me, wincing her blistered foot into a high heel shoe.
    She held the other shoe up to my face,
        pointing at the 4 inches—*you can use a stiletto
to drive into a man's eye if you need to.* Lipstick on her teeth
    like she'd eaten a heart. And no one knew
        who killed her. The parents, the brother, a faceless
man entering through the window. She looked like a little doll I got
    for Christmas, never taken out of the box. My mother
        cooed at her curls, folded the magazine so I could see
the dead beauty queen—asked if I wanted
    my hair to look just like hers. The day the boys found us,
        we were in the boatyard. Their fists
clenched as we retreated, trapped by the fence and shoreline. Cornered.
    I picked up a rusted blade used to saw barnacles off the bottoms

of boats. I didn't know much but I knew how to growl loud,
       my mouth foaming, mad as a feral cat,
              I knew how to say, *I'll cut your throats.* My bony limbs
       waving, wild and dangerous   *jeeze, it's just a game*
shaking their heads, leaving me there—Amy too—
       never looked at me
           the same way again.

Nightshade

for Amy

She called me the morning after—
hair brambled into a nest, her eyes
an upshot of so-what—to tell me
that after bottles clinked out of his father's
liquor cabinet, they fucked in every

room. And she broke open forgetting
to count the days of her cycle. Her hips
a burst of red snarl all over the house.
The sofa, the kitchen, his parents'
bedroom: a trophy of defiance they grinned

through as she puddled, unaware of the blood
anchoring out of her. And when the sun rose
he called her *bitch* for the stains on his mother's
linens. Teardrop shapes sloping from where
she was bent over the armchair. Thick

fingerprints purpling on the counter. She called me
and I appeared there in this instance of morning,
arms heavy with jugs of cleaning agent.

She led me to the deepest mark of her, a nightshade,
a bodiless heart imprinted on an eggshell
duvet. And it was something ancient,

the way we took a knee and began
to scrub. Grinning into each other, dipping
rags into cups of bleach. Why wouldn't
this be as natural as saying our own names?
As if we weren't familiar with this kind of slow
removal. As if we didn't already know how
to clean ourselves out of the world.

Climate

It felt familiar, your mouth moving
        up my side like a gale warning. My
                arm calico, *mammatus* clouds,
        blood brought to the surface.
Now, I understand my childhood
        home. Releasing shingle after shingle
                into the brutal air. Our front door
        torn and flat in the yard. Violent
gusts whipping through the marshes—
        the back of your hand.
                Of what I have unlearned,
        this was the hardest.
One sandpiper singing
        still, desire does not
                have to leave you
                        ruined.

Light from Years and Years Ago

I made nothing of my leaving. Baseball glove grease
slicked on the hinges. My bed shaped to look like a body
sleeping. Slipping out onto the small stage of night.
He was waiting for me with a bottle of vodka.

This was the summer I took to running and wheezed
my way to the edge of town, stopped by the bay, the ocean,
the interstate. Cornered. He told me things I already knew
about the stars, how the light

was old. I cooed in surprise anyway, the bottle stuck
in the sand between us, as quiet as a chess piece.
My hips were new, so I gave myself a new name.
Said I was born somewhere else, smiled, lied
about my age, lied about—

        When I wake it's morning. Salt crusting
my eyelashes shut. Alone and half
in the tide, my panties rough with a handful
of sand. As I rise,

the seagulls startle, shocked by my living. Wings
springing away from the driftwood. I stumble
home. And it's different

after that. Which is to say, it's no longer a lie
to say *yes* when my father asks if I remember
that one time when a tiger shark

washed ashore. How it was stiff on the sand
and everyone stood in a circle around it. How I,
three years old, slinked through the crowd, toddled over
to the dead thing—kissed it on its nose.

Relapse

swaddled in souring bedsheets, soiled and blessed by the christ-light
    of her television, I find her each time wrapped in on herself
        like a spool of unused yarn. My mother is five days on nothing

but pills I can tell from the chalk of her mouth, cracked along the corners
    her gut-fish lips shaping something of a prayer, over and over again
        so quietly nothing could hear it but her own ghost unwinding

out of her eyes thrown upward and my empty slap, slap, of her slack-jawed
    cheek bringing her back to the surprise of me. Her face is a twisted knot
        searching for who I am, sifting out the familiar pieces

of me and I am hollowing, unrecognized by the confused beauty I grew
    out of, she is reaching for me, holding, mumbling a louder limpness
        unscrewing like a cork with a mouthful of wordless

please, please owling and slurring through the sharpness of her body—a frozen
    birch tree filled with birds who broke their beaks one by one against
        the windows trying to hear what she was saying and I am trying

to hear what she is saying—but the dog came back from the dead
    through all her howling when she looked at me, child again,
        calling me *mommy, mommy, mommy.*

The Addict's Daughter Speaks to Addiction

It hasn't gone unnoticed. You have been kinder
            to us. Haven't pushed her too far, didn't keep her
    unconscious in the snow for very long—thank you.

I am as much your child, showing me when
            to let her sleep through the afternoon, how to make
    my own dinner. There are moments I forget I was not born

of you. I see how you part her lips for the bottle, rerouting
            the car to the liquor store each time forcing her hand
    into a fistful of my hair begging *oh god no*
as I pour each one down the drain. I know

            how you take the shape of almost anything:
    an empty fridge, dead houseplants.
In this way, we aren't different:
            my cheekbones caving into hers
    when you tuck the hair behind my ear,
whenever you wash a week of my life blank

as paper. And when my hands shake in the morning,
    I see how you love something new.
You are all legacy, a need asleep inside me.
        This singular hunger, as long as
my life, larger each day. I know you

    could do worse and have not. Thank you
for not taking everything. Thank you for leaving me
            this white-nightgown ghost washing
    the same dish over and over again. A woman
who clings to the floor like a shipwreck, calling me
            by my grandmother's name, asking for it

    to be over. Look. There is nothing
left, just this woman's moth-eaten mind. Isn't that enough?

What else? What do you need?
What can I give you more of?

The Ocean's Constant Moving

So often it was only us. My mother and I, held together
       in the rain-sick dark.
She'd ask me to sleep on my father's side
       of the bed. The steady hum
of the television. Reliable. The weather
       channel and its heat map. A storm
and all the shades of red it might be. How much longer
       until our home needed to be raised on stilts?
Our shoreline less and less each year. Only us. My mother's
       hand in mine twitching in that way a body resists
sleep. A small S.O.S from the nervous
       system as we curled in and away from
each other in the fitful half-dawn. The light
       from the bathroom left on. My mother startling
awake, clawing at the air, gasping as if trapped underwater.
       Once, in a small murmur—half awake,
my girl, my girl, this life, it's hell. My dreams
       and the dog clicking her way down the hall.
Sleepless. We'd rise and wander the house
       in shifts. The groan of the bed when
she would return. And then I'd wake to shuffle
       from room to room, stepping into the shadows
cast into our home by the ocean's constant
       moving.

To My Assailant, Years Later

The water has gnawed our beach
into a little hangnail cliff. Can you believe it?
The gumless smile of something defanged. That's all.

When I return, it's winter and the snow keeps the ground
frozen together. A gull's wing stiff in the sand—as cold
as a moon. And I hate

that it's gone. The place where it happened.
It means I am what is left. I am what can't be
weathered away. I try

to think about forgiveness. How the ocean accepts
the wrecks we give it. But that's not true. Not really.
Although, I have seen

the way sunken ships soften into reefs. Foliage floating
off steel. A violence turned into a home.
I don't even remember your name. I have forgotten

so much in the act of continuing to live.
I do remember that you were just a boy. And I can see how
I looked to you. How I couldn't be a girl

who woke at dawn to lead restless horses into a wildflower
field. Or a girl who sang off key. A girl whose mother
was always drifting away from her. I couldn't be anything

real. So I wasn't. Not for years. And what I don't remember
does not haunt me. But still, my mouth tightens when I fade
into thought. I wake up afraid, pushing away

empty air. Your jawline, rising up like steady barnacle
growth in my mind. Hard, calcified—a tooth
out of nowhere. Still, I look for you in the smiles

of men. But this, you must already know. And that's not why
I am here. On this beach. I came because I want you to know
what happened afterwards. I want you to know about the change

in my mother. After that day, the bruises you left, the thought of you
thick in the air gave her a mooring able to latch to me.
And just for a moment the gulf between my mother and I

was gone when she looked at me—*my god*—for the first time
like I finally understood.

Delta

After they married my mother moved
into his house. My father laughs
about the girl she was. He likes to recall her
first mistakes: high heels in the horse barn,
press-on nails while learning to splice
rope, hairspray by a wood stove.
The refusal to gut a fish. I don't remember
these tiny failures; only my mother
chasing possums from our porch steps,
digging oysters out of the shoreline—
eating them raw—hiding the love letters
other women would send my father
like she was born to do it.

The Relief

When the bedsheets wouldn't bleach white again, there was something
to be unearthed. Loose pills spilling from the dirty laundry,
a bottle of vodka tucked back under the sink and my hollow mother
set sleeping as I yanked the relief from each room: removing
the stash she kept inside the piano, a fifth of liquor rolling out of each
shoebox, an unprescribed fistful from her sock drawer. Everything
was thrush with her wanting, thick with the terror of being left

without. When she woke   to the house defanged
          I heard her spin each drawer open
to emptiness   yelping   wild
lapping   at the vinegar   the mouthwash gulped
   down until she found that one thing
I missed   then quiet.   And nothing
          but the temperature dropping fast
and the pipes clanking in reply.

   It was the cold that pulled me
from my bed to find the sliding door shouldered open, and a tiny crest
          of weather banking up on the living room rug.
There was a trail in the knee-deep snow
   from where she fled the lack, stepping like a bride into the blue
          darkness of morning, robe blown open, one barefoot stride
at a time.   I followed it,

          found her fallen by the tree where the dead dog's chain grew
into the bark and the winter hid the dirt circle where the animal's
living had killed the grass permanently. I could hear her thin clouds
          of breathing, the fluttering of the whites of her eyes,
   her pink thighs tucked up into her mouth clenched *goddamnit* shut
and through all the shivering her body somehow bucking *no, no* against the will
          that brought her there.

Is this how you go? And shame shocked through me before looping
my arms under hers, plowing a thick line with her body, my own

bare feet purple, as I dragged her inside, drew her
a bath, undid the flint of her leaving: the pills, the vodka—
everything—I put back.

Policy

At the rehab center, she carries her whole jewelry box inside
      with her luggage. A large, ruby case,   rabid and foaming
      with pearls.

Shuffling through the intake procedures, her eyes are heavy and hateful
      from weeks of escape.   I hold her coat as they pat her
      down. Searching

          for what isn't allowed. Gloved hands parting
the silks of her suitcase.   *No.*   *Not the jewelry.*
      Can't be held responsible if anything goes missing.

She clutches the box to her chest,
      one necklace snaking to the floor.   *It's policy*
they apologize   but I talk them into letting her keep three pairs

          of earrings. So we sit on the linoleum floor,
the box—an open heart between us—as she reaches in,
      holding each   pair up to her cheek. Her eye
bruised
      from falling down the stairs, a thin crust of blood
in the corner of her lip.   Doctors and nurses step
      around us as she asks me, each time.
      This one?   *This one?*   *Tell me.*
      Do I look beautiful?

On Keeping a Pet

My mother's girlhood ponytail
was kept in plastic in the bottom drawer
where the good china was stored
but never used.

It was my pet slipped free
into my lap. Soft fray of auburn
I'd run my hand along.

I never tried to imagine her
face as the hair was severed.
That slow cascade grasped in the fist
of the blade holder.

The offerings I'd bring to it were always
ignored. Handwritten letters, strawberry
jellybeans. A very quiet song.

What Can't Be Cut from Us

Each home twisted with the architecture of grief.
    The staircases of widow's walks ribboned up
        to every roof. Our skyline was embroidered

with want—splintered
    platforms wide enough for just
        one woman. This is what came before:

men gone out to sea, their wives pressed against
    the banisters for years. Each one damp
        with lamp-oil, crisp with waiting. Now, they sit empty

and eaten by salt, crowning each home
    with a chipped rotting. One stacked
        with a rusted mass of air-conditioners. Others

hoarded with gull nests. Teenagers climbed
    them, the cherries of their cigarettes glowing
        from across the pond. Mine too. Extended

from my window, had grown soft
    with mold. Lines of ivy curling around
        a damp swelling.

A hazard—the county
    declared and called for its removal.
        The day it happened, the whole town came

to watch. An industrial crane hummed
    around our house for hours, breaking
        the beams with a metal scathing. Everyone

whooped and cheered for the dismantling.
    Squeals of peeling layer after layer, as
        we shed what clung to our home.

That night, my window—bright
    and empty—kept me awake. The salt air thick
        as I rose to get a glass of water. And I saw her.

My mother in the yard. Her nightgown soaking up
    the swamp. Her arms outstretched as she waited
        and waited and waited for something to return.

Awaiting the Elegy

answering the phone expecting each time
she's dead, she's dead, goddamnit—

for my mother, whose room I enter like a zoo
cage, ready for the smell of a body forgotten.

A bag packed under my bed, I look
for the notice in the paper, a small story

about what not-living does to a hardwood floor.
I can tell you how addiction spills outward, nine

opossum nests thickening around our gutters,
the damn soil rank, nothing grows. And me.

I am flooding with beautiful things
I can't say about her. An elegy calcified

in my throat. Who taught me this?
How to gather up grief

like a bouquet in waltzing preparation—
it's what I know. Forgive me, forgive me,

 I am waiting.

The Dove

Not uncommon for a city to be full of fled things.
This bird, with her half crushed skull. One foot
permanently balled into a lace of barbed-wire,
beaking mites from a wing growing out of its clip.

I know her story. Escaped from the hands of an amateur
magician, battered, learning to be wild, mistaking
a plastic bag for another tortured thing. She is a symbol

for peace—but I know better. On my window-
ledge for days. Feathers white as surrender, cooing
like a pot of boiling water as the butcher shop below
buzzes back its constant

slaughter. It is my lamp-light she huddles
into. And what I could see in her—the way she was pulled
out of a pocket and tossed into the air. The gnarled grip
of his fist yanking her up, cupping her body flightless,

covering her cage with a dark, damp cloth. But now,
our bodies on either side of the glass. Her one good
eye finding mine.

Acknowledgements

I am deeply grateful to the editors of the journals in which these poems, or earlier versions of these poems, first appeared.

Academy of American Poets, Poem-a-Day (poets.org) – "Climate"
Adroit Journal – "Portrait of Mother as Gone"
Day One – "The Addict's Daughter Speaks to Addiction"
Cumberland River Review – "When Princess Diana Died"
Foundry – "On Keeping a Pet"
Indiana Review – "Researchers Find that Trauma is Inherited Through DNA"
The Missouri Review – "Field Trip" "South County, Matunuck, RI," "Wild and
       Dangerous" "To My Assailant, 15 Years Later," "Awaiting the Elegy," "The Dove"
Narrative Magazine – "Gaslight"
Nimrod Journal – "The Relief"
North American Review – "Infestation"
The Paris-American– "Delta"
Pleiades – "My Mother Tells Me About Her Assault"
storySouth – "On Keeping a Pet"
Tinderbox – "Light from Years and Years Ago"
Washington Square Review – "Nightshade"

This chapbook would not be possible without the support of Jeff McDaniel who made (and continues to make) Sarah Lawrence College a magical place for emerging poets. Who told me to start going to Al-Anon meetings, which undoubtedly saved my life.

Thank you to my MFA cohort, particularly John McCarthy, Anna Knowles, Drew Hemmert, and Jacqui Zeng. And for my professors Judy Jordan, Allison Joseph, and Jon Tribble.

Thank you to the members of that very special poetry class at Sarah Lawrence College, small and intimate and booming with raw talent––the reason I continued to write. Thank you to Aja Monet for her passion and drive and heart, which has always inspired me. Thank you to Ava Winter for her gorgeous lens, her powerful words. Thank you to Juniper Waller for her joy in art that she shares generously.

Thank you to The Wizard Brett Bevel, Helena Kadir, and their Little Wizard Dylan. Thank you to Omega Institute for glowing with energy and giving me a creative home.

Thank you to Taneum Bambrick for reading this manuscript in an earlier version and pushing it forward with her smart and insightful notes.

Thank you to Megan Falley for her genius online classes and her kind blurb of this book.

Thank you to Krista Vernoff for taking a chance on me and believing in my writing and my story.

Thank you to Shayfer James, who lived through the poems with me and was their first reader. Thank you to my sister Melyssa Plunket-Gomez for always giving me her attic to write in. Thank you to Arndt Peemoeller for meeting the sharp pieces of me through these poems with grace and love.

Thank you to anyone that has ever touched my life with poetry, I am eternally changed and deeply grateful.

And thank you to my mother, the maypole of these poems. My mother who is a brave, raw nerve and who did her best to protect me from the inevitable hold of the world. Thank you for my life and for your beautiful, brambled journey to harbor.

MEGHANN PLUNKETT writes television (Station 19, Rebel) and various development projects including adapting the novel "First Lie Wins" for the screen. She also served as a Poetry Reader for *The New Yorker* from 2018-2020. She is the recipient of the 2017 *Missouri Review*'s Editors' Prize as well as the 2017 *Third Coast* Poetry Prize. She was a finalist for *Narrative Magazine's* 30 Below Contest, *The North American Review*'s Hearst Poetry Prize and *Nimrod*'s Pablo Neruda Prize. She has been recognized by the Academy of American Poets in both 2016 and 2017. Her work can be found or is forthcoming in *Best New Poets*, *Pleiades*, *Rattle*, *Washington Square Review* and *Poets.org*, among others.

www.ingramcontent.com/pod-product-compliance
Lightning Source LLC
Chambersburg PA
CBHW031542040426

42445CB00010B/657